The ^New Compleat
FACILITATOR
a handbook for facilitators

HOWICK ASSOCIATES

DREW HOWICK
STUART DAILY
ABBY SPRIK

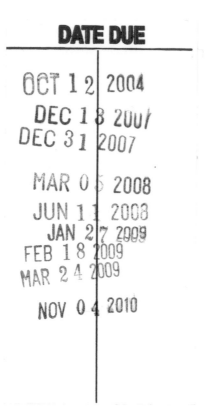
ISBN 0-9646972-1-1

Phone: 800-236-3370

Web: www.howickassociates.com

Printed in the United States

DEDICATION

In 1994, the original edition of *The Compleat Facilitator* was published. We received all sorts of feedback, compliments and inquiries about the work, including notification that we had misspelled a word in the title! In response we referred our readers to the dedication, which referenced a book written by Izaak Walton in 1653, *The Compleat Angler*. As we stated in 1994, "Although nominally about fishing, the book is still regarded as the seminal work on the uses of recreation by the people of England. Most reviewers consider the work witty and comprehensive. By selecting the name *The Compleat Facilitator*, we salute Walton and we hope the work is similarly witty and comprehensive."

Facilitation skills are essential for anyone who wishes to help groups of people engage in productive conversations. Many things need to be present for this to happen: Desire, interest, timing, and interpersonal chemistry certainly play a part. What is also needed is an understanding of facilitation principles, and their successful application. When carefully applied, these principles will enable facilitators to accomplish extraordinary results in their work with groups. It is to those people that we dedicate this work.

ACKNOWLEDGMENTS

Shortly after our sixth printing of *The Compleat Facilitator*, a colleague suggested that our book was dated. Acknowledging the 1994 publishing date, we pondered the possibility. Can practical advice on group process be dated? I thought not, yet wondered if it was as COMPLETE as it could be. Could the work be enhanced? Did the work need a facelift? A minor tuck? Major surgery?

Compared to eight years ago, my colleagues and I have more experience and knowledge about group effectiveness and the impact that a skilled facilitator can make. What we didn't know was if our readers thought an updated version was needed. What to do? "Time for a focus group!" I exclaimed. Twenty-seven people familiar with the book agreed to share their opinions, preferences and desires for a "new and improved." They told us what they liked about the book, ways to enhance it and how it might be better organized. Their contributions were invaluable. I would like to thank Jon Bales, Deforest Area School District; David Birren, State of Wisconsin, Department of Natural Resources; Sara Burr, Department of Natural Resources; Ruth Gonsky, BNY Clearing Services; Rhonda Holler, US Cellular; Mike Miller, CUNA & Affiliates; Palmira Minta, Fiserv; Mary Beth Petersen, Children's Hospital of Wisconsin; Pam Peterson, Lands' End; Tim Poshek (retired), Journal Communication; Michelle Primus, Direct Supply; Dan Prueher, Datex-Ohmeda; Trish Rensink, North Arizona University; Joe Sensenbrenner, Sensenbrenner Associates; Rachel Stanton, WE Energies; Kerwin Steffen, Kerwin Steffen Associates; Bert Stitt, Bert Stitt Associates; Marilyn Westmas, Berbee; Geoff Wheeler, State of Wisconsin, WHEDA; Barbara Wolf-Shousha, BNY Clearing Services; and Jody Zanton, Johnson Controls, Inc.

The contributions of these individuals built on the original work of a number of talented people. Barry Roberts and Kevin Upton are the original "parents" of the first edition and I would like to thank them and the original cast of forty who shared their ideas with us eight years ago. Those that took the lead on this edition are Stuart Daily and Abby Sprik, both of whom are skilled facilitators. I commend their ability to find the time between "real work" facilitation projects and staying focused on the WHO and WHY for this book. Our in-house sounding boards and content contributors included Jeff Hanan and Mal Jeffris, both of whom bring a great deal of facilitation expertise to bear. My thanks to staff member Rebecca Fischer for her eye for detail and Lori Heiking for her ideas and energetic belief that EVERYBODY should possess a copy of the book!

Although Victoria Jones is not a member of our staff, there were times when she appeared to be! Her contributions to this work were many and significant. Vicky took our many ideas, experiences, anecdotes (and illusions) and somehow found the right words and made the necessary connections.

Other individuals that I would like to thank for their efforts are Jay Rath, for sharing his creative talent by providing the original illustrations, Steve Stanczyk for his expertise in graphic design and his never ending supply of practical ideas for organizing the material, and Laurie Joiner for her encouragement and peer review of the book.

Bringing together the talents and energy of all these people was my job. The task included the seeking of opinions, the collecting of experiences, the connecting of ideas, and the collaboration of those who cared about producing a useful work. In short, the facilitation of a challenging and rewarding process, that has resulted in what I hope the reader finds useful.

Drew Howick

TABLE OF CONTENTS

CHAPTER 1 - THE FACILITATOR'S JOB

The Wisdom of Groups 2

Benefits of a Facilitated Process 3

Building a Climate for Meaningful Conversation 4

Encouraging Active Participation 7

Guiding the Group Through Decision-Making 7

Helping the Group Track Its Progress 8

What If 10

Pitfalls to Avoid 11

CHAPTER 2 - THE GROUP'S JOB

Understanding the Role of the Group Leader 14

   - Helping the Group Understand Its Job 15

Defining the Next Steps 16

   - Setting Goals and Milestones 17

What If 18

Pitfalls to Avoid 19

CHAPTER 3 - PREPARING TO FACILITATE

Having the Right Frame of Mind 22

Why Meet? 22

Why Plan? 23

The Agenda 25

   - Setting Objectives 25

   - Building the Agenda 26

What If 30

Pitfalls to Avoid 31

TABLE OF CONTENTS

CHAPTER 4 - MANAGING MEETINGS

Facilitating Meetings 34

Opening the Meeting 35

    - The Check-in 35

Reviewing the Agenda and Process 36

Assigning Responsibilities 36

The Power of the Pen 37

Creating Ground Rules 38

Keeping the Group Focused and Moving Forward 41

    - The Parking Lot 43

Closing the Meeting 45

    - The Check-out 45

Tips for Teleconference Meetings 46

What If 47

Pitfalls to Avoid 49

CHAPTER 5 - IDEA GENERATION

Generating and Sorting Ideas 52

    - Guidelines for Idea Generation 52

    - Brainstorming 54

    - Brainwriting 56

    - Affinity Process 57

Decision-Making 58

    - Consensus-Building 58

    - Multi-voting 59

    - Decision Matrix 61

    - Quick-Check-Why 62

What If 64

Pitfalls to Avoid 65

TABLE OF CONTENTS

CHAPTER 6 - PLANNING & IMPLEMENTATION

The Facilitator's Role...68

Determining the Next Steps...68

    - Flowchart...69

    - Tree Diagram...69

Contingency Planning...70

    - Troll Search...70

    - Force Field Analysis...71

    - Contingency Diagram...72

Establishing Responsibility..72

    - Decision Matrix...73

What If...74

Pitfalls to Avoid...75

CHAPTER 7 - DEALING WITH DIFFICULT BEHAVIORS

Unproductive Behavior..78

    - When and Why it Happens..78

How to Enforce Ground Rules..79

Working Through Conflict...82

    - When and Why it Happens..82

Pitfalls to Avoid...84

Index...87

THE NEW COMPLEAT FACILITATOR

Who should read this book

You might be a group member, a group leader, or an individual convening a group. Or maybe you've had some facilitation experience and even some facilitation training, but still consider yourself a novice. You could be a manager or group leader who wants to understand how facilitation can help your group. Or you're a group sponsor interested in knowing what skills to look for when hiring a professional facilitator. If you are involved with a group that wants to get something done, we wrote this book for you.

You might be asking yourself why a consulting firm that specializes in providing group process facilitation wants everyone to learn facilitation. Aren't we inviting you to put us out of business by teaching you what we do? In fact, groups whose members and leaders understand how groups work and how they can best participate are the groups we like to work with best!

The best facilitator for your group may be someone from outside the group, a trained facilitator who has absolutely no stake in the decisions your group will be making. But we also recognize that bringing in a professional facilitator might be beyond your means. Some alternatives include:

- Selecting a group member to facilitate

- Having the group leader take on the facilitator role

- Rotating the facilitator job so that every group member has the opportunity to facilitate *and* participate throughout the process

- Recruiting someone from another area of the organization to facilitate

Where facilitation is useful

Facilitation is a good approach if your group wants to…

- Use its time efficiently

- Make well informed decisions

- Reach its goals more quickly

- Promote full participation from its members

- Resolve issues and solve problems

- Define goals and set objectives

- Generate ideas

- Bring the right resources to an issue

- Share feelings and opinions

- Keep group discussion on track

- Keep records of what it's doing

- Build skills and foster leadership

- Support the contributions of its members

Why everyone needs facilitation skills

Every group can benefit from a facilitative approach. When everyone is committed to the success of the group, supporting the facilitative process just makes good sense, whether one is playing the role of facilitator or participating in the process. Having everyone aligned with the principles and techniques of facilitation—full cooperation, open and respectful communication, shared decision-making, mutual responsibility, and shared power—makes every facilitator's job easier.

What you will learn from reading this book

We wrote this book to help you…

- Understand the nature of group dynamics

- Recognize and foster productive group behavior

- Build facilitative skills in yourself and your group

- Prepare yourself, mentally and emotionally, for the challenge of facilitating a group

- Guide your group through the process of defining issues, generating ideas, and making informed decisions

- Plan and facilitate meetings

- Troubleshoot difficult situations

- Begin building a toolbox of techniques to assist the group in its work

How to use The Compleat Facilitator

We've organized this book as both a handbook and a workbook, intending it to be practical and easy to use. It's structured to guide you through the process of building your knowledge about facilitating successful group work from beginning to end.

Read *The Compleat Facilitator* through to prepare for facilitation. Then use it as an aid while you are facilitating. This new edition of *The Compleat Facilitator* was designed to be a quick and easy resource.

Take it with you to meetings as a quick reference. Write in the margins. Flag the sections you refer to most often with sticky notes. Share it with other members of your group, your boss, your group's sponsor, and anyone who has a stake in the work you are doing.

We've learned a lot since we released the first edition of *The Compleat Facilitator* in 1994. This edition combines what we've learned with what we've heard from our clients about what made the original an indispensable resource for them.

We wanted to make this edition of *The Compleat Facilitator* even more practical and accessible than the first (of which we are still very proud, by the way).

We hope that what you find in these pages will help you navigate the waters of facilitation with confidence. Let us know how we did. Our address is:

Howick Associates
111 N. Fairchild Street
Madison, WI 53703
info@howickassociates.com

CHAPTER 1

THE FACILITATOR'S JOB

Topics covered by this chapter

■ The benefits of a facilitated process.

■ The facilitator's role in managing the process.

■ Strategies for maximizing individual contributions.

The Wisdom of Groups

Definitions

Process: How a group handles information, makes decisions, and takes action.

Content: The information, decisions, and actions the group handles, makes, and takes.

We can call them groups, teams, task forces, committees, families, clubs, unions, congregations, crews, boards, or councils. Their members can be volunteers, recruits, or veterans. Whatever their name and composition, when people gather to put their diverse opinions, experiences, insights, talents, and energies to the task of accomplishing a goal together, magic can happen. When group work is going well, information flows, ideas multiply, creativity flourishes, productivity increases, and community strengthens.

A group can accomplish more than an individual can because it has more resources available for solving a problem or getting a job done. People working together generate more ideas than people working separately because they can inspire and energize one another. A group is more likely to find innovative solutions for problems because it fosters creativity and reduces individual risk. Group work can enhance receptiveness toward organizational changes because the group plays a part in determining the direction of the changes. Participants in successful group work can emerge from the process with a stronger dedication to organizational goals and a sense of community with one another.

We at Howick Associates believe in the wisdom of groups. We witness its magic every day, in the facilitation work we do with our corporate clients to the synergies we see in our own staff meetings.

We've also seen how group work can go awry. Even the best-intentioned groups can be short-circuited by power struggles, muddy communications, conflicting roles, unclear goals, and hidden agendas. Plans can get stonewalled, feelings can get hurt, and time and money can get wasted.

Howick Associates is in the business of helping groups succeed. And we've observed that one difference between groups that succeed and groups that stumble is that successful group leaders and members understand the nature of groups, the difference between productive and unproductive group behaviors, and some basic approaches to facilitating the group process.

Benefits of a Facilitated Process

The word *facilitate* has its origin in the Latin word *facilis*, which means "easy." Group work is made easier by the contributions of a *facilitator*.

As facilitator, you are the one member of the group who, when the group is working together, doesn't participate in the decision-making process. Your main concern is how effectively group members work together to produce results, rather than exactly what results the group will produce. Your job is to facilitate the *process*.

Key to a facilitator's success is neutrality and objectivity toward the *content* with which the group is working. The facilitator is the person who worries about the *how* and must therefore remain neutral about the *what*.

The reason for this is that a group will do its best work only if it remains open to all variety of ideas, information, and opinions. The chances of a group accomplishing this are improved if there is an unbiased individual safeguarding the process who is not involved in the group's decision. As facilitator, your unbiased stance reduces internal politics and creates opportunities for all ideas to be heard, even the unpopular ones.

Your focus on process will free the group members to put their complete energy into dealing with the issues at hand. Your attention to stretching the group's information-gathering and idea-generating efforts will prevent "group-think."

About "process"

We've been telling you that a facilitator concerns him/herself with "process," that is, *how* a group gets its work done. A well-planned process allows the group to:

- Stay focused

- Make progress

- Generate ideas

- Solve problems

- Make decisions

- Manage conflict

The facilitator helps the group accomplish this by:

- Building a climate for meaningful conversation

- Encouraging active participation

- Guiding the group through decision-making

- Helping the group track its progress by observing and providing feedback

The process is one of full cooperation, open and respectful communication, shared decision-making, and mutual responsibility. In a facilitated process power is shared and consensus-building is fundamental.

Building a Climate for Meaningful Conversation

Survey the environment

Group work often happens in the context of a larger organization, even if the "organization" is an informal one, such as family members or a group of friends. When you understand the group's personality and politics, you will be able to choose the most effective tools and techniques for working with the group.

Throughout the process, stay alert to those aspects of the group's dynamics that will have an impact on members' willingness and ability to communicate openly and honestly. Keep an open mind – what you thought was true at first glance may prove to be otherwise later on.

Things to look for:

- Which members seem to have the most/least authority in the outside world?

- Which members seem to have the most/least influence?

- Which members seem to have the most/least expertise about the project on which the group will be working?

- What are the politics of the larger organization?

- How successful have teams been in the past?

- How has the larger organization dealt with change in the past?

- Any land mines or potholes? Skeletons in the closet?

Setting the stage

To communicate openly and honestly, group members need:

...Permission

Group members need to know that it's all right to bring up an idea or a concern, even if it causes disagreement or tension. Give them permission by:

- Modeling, with your own behavior, open and honest communication.

- Clarifying how issues or problems should be brought up for discussion.

- Allowing time for sharing concerns in each meeting.

...Respect

The fear of feeling stupid, silly, or little can make people keep their thoughts to themselves. Build a climate of respect by:

- Modeling thoughtful listening yourself, reflecting back what people say so that they know they've been heard.

- Acknowledging and valuing all contributions.

- Keeping the conversation focused on issues, not individuals.

- Developing ground rules that prohibit attacking, ridiculing, interrupting, and use of disrespectful body language.

...Accessibility

People have different ways of processing information and communicating what's on their mind. Some can speak quickly and off-the-cuff; others need time to reflect. Some people learn through what they hear; others learn through their experiences. Some express themselves verbally; others feel more articulate when they can write things down. Make it easy for everyone in the group to contribute by:

- Restating what you hear for people to hear again.

- Encouraging participants to ask for clarification when they need it.

- Reading written input out loud for people to hear.

- Posting items on a flip chart or board for people to read.

- Providing pads, sticky notes, and pencils for everyone before a meeting.

- Making sure that meeting decisions are recapped in writing.

- Encouraging people to get up and walk around during meetings if it helps them think.

...Confidence

People need to feel competent to handle the issues on which the group is working. Help group members build confidence in their combined brains, talents, experience, and energy by:

- Making sure that everyone understands and can articulate the group's mission.

- Having the group build an inventory of all the skills and talents present in the group.

- Providing a variety of opportunities for fact-collecting and idea-generation.

- Encouraging members to contribute in their areas of expertise.

Lighten Up

The one important thing I have learned over the years is the difference between taking one's work seriously and taking one's self seriously. The first is imperative and the second is disastrous.

-Margot Fonteyn

...Meaning

Group members need to feel that speaking up is worth the trouble and will make a difference. Show them how their input contributes to the group's progress by:

- Asking for input from the group and from individuals.

- Recording *all* input on a flip chart or board.

- Thanking people for their input.

- Building follow-through on input, suggestions, and issues into the group's next steps.

Encouraging Active Participation

The reason to invite an individual into a group is that his/her participation in discussions and interaction with other group members is vital to the group's success. One of the challenges is balancing participation and managing the discussion to ensure that each group member has an equal opportunity to contribute. Group members who monopolize the discussion or inhibit others from participating can undermine the group's cohesiveness. Involve every one by:

- Structuring discussion to produce input from each group member.

- Giving people quiet time to think and write down their ideas before sharing them with the group.

- Building fun into the process and acknowledging everyone's input.

- Working with group members individually to identify and overcome barriers to their participation.

- Making sure that no one is dominating the process.

Guiding the Group Through Decision-Making

A group's work will be most effective if it first determines a *structured process* for decision-making before it begins to determine what decisions need to be made. Chapter Five describes some ways for helping the group choose and prioritize ideas.

Whether you are deciding on a list of ground rules or tackling a large, complex problem, using a structured decision-making process helps your group:

- Generate ideas and identify options.

- Make choices without feeling overwhelmed by details.

- Minimize decision-making based on emotions.

- Assess the strengths and weaknesses of every idea.

- Build and reach consensus.

- Articulate the rationale behind the decisions it makes.

Helping the Group Track its Progress by Observing and Giving Feedback

The group needs to know how it's doing. Make sure you spend time observing *how* the group is working together and communicating. Share your observations with them frequently. The objective, constructive feedback you offer during the process helps the group reflect upon how well the work is progressing. Feedback is a two-way street. In addition to providing feedback, it is important to regularly solicit feedback from group members. Don't assume that, because nobody has said anything, everything is going well. People need to be asked.

Feedback can be as formal as a survey or as casual as a check-out at the end of a meeting.

Check points for feedback

During the process the facilitator should assess:

- How well is the process working?

- Are we adhering to ground rules?

- Is there open communication?

- Is there balanced participation?

- Are we having meaningful conversations?

- Is the group accomplishing its mission?

It ain't a bad plan to keep still occasionally, even when you know what you're talking about.

-Kin Hubbard

At the end of a meeting:

- Did we achieve our meeting objectives?

- Did we stay on track?

- Did we honor our ground rules?

- What should we do differently next time?

Evaluating the facilitator

Don't assume that you can see what you're doing. You need to ask the group members how they feel about your work and what the opportunities are for improvement. Are you:

- Planning well?

- Keeping communication open and flowing?

- Keeping the group on track?

- Sticking to the process?

- Adjusting the process when warranted?

Outcomes of a good process

A well-facilitated group should excel at:

- Working collaboratively and cooperatively

- Exchanging information

- Solving problems

- Generating ideas

- Making high quality decisions

- Developing a plan for implementation

Remembering to not take yourself too seriously is a good maxim for life, as well as for facilitation. Don't walk into every facilitation expecting to slay dragons. Expect, however, that you will be human, with all of the foibles and frailties that are part of the human package. If you forgive yourself for being imperfect, so will your group. Don't forget to forgive the group its imperfections, as well.

Never underestimate the value of a good laugh!

When things go awry – which happens in facilitation as well as in life – keep your perspective. Don't take it as a judgment of your worth as a human being. Rather, step back from it enough that you and the group can learn from it.

9

What If...	Try...
...it feels like I'm being asked to be the group leader instead of the facilitator?	...clarifying the difference between the two roles. Refer to Chapter 2 for more information on roles.
...I have a stake in the issue this group is working on?	...explaining your interest in the topic to the group.
...there are lots of personal agendas?	...posting the group's mission in clear view for every meeting.
...the group doesn't know how to communicate openly?	...asking the group to share their hopes and concerns about working together. ...using the tools in Chapter 3 to help participants express their opinions.
...this is my first facilitation experience?	...making sure you understand: -your role -the desired outcomes -the dynamics of the group ...being open and honest yourself! Tell the group, and ask for its help/support.
...my only facilitation tools are brainstorming and informal discussion?	...using them when they are appropriate, but remember that they are limited. Learn and use more facilitation techniques throughout the process.

Pitfalls to avoid

✔ Relying only on processes that require participant's verbal skills. Significant contributions can be missed if you don't accommodate those who are less verbal.

✔ Assuming that lack of participation means not contributing. Contributions to a group come in many ways, some of which are more subtle, but none-the-less, valuable.

✔ Inconsistent recognition of member's contributions. "Good idea" to one and not to another can be interpreted as evaluative and may unintentionally influence future contributions.

✔ Allowing the problem-solving process to be altered or changed in order to save time may provide a short-term fix, but not a long-term solution.

✔ Allowing the group to avoid assessing their effectiveness. Adequate time for the group to reflect on how they are doing may have a significant impact on the process and group dynamics.

THE GROUP'S JOB

Topics covered by this chapter

- Understanding the group's job.
- Helping the group understand its job.
- Defining the next steps.

Understanding the Role of the Group Leader

Never go into a facilitation without understanding why the group exists and why you've been asked to facilitate its work. This clarification process usually begins by talking to the group leader.

The *group leader* has the authority to direct the group's efforts, assemble the resources it needs, and report its decisions and actions to the sponsor, if there is one. He/she can be designated as group leader by the sponsor, or selected by the group.

The group leader is responsible for ensuring that the group does its job. As someone with a stake in the outcome, it is important that the group leader be able to participate fully in the group's work, voicing opinions and ideas, providing input, contributing to the decision-making, and taking on assignments along with his/her teammates. The group leader influences the group's work by communicating the sponsor's interests to the group, helping the facilitator plan and manage meetings, and representing the team within the larger organization.

Prior to the First Meeting with the Group Leader, You Should...

...Define the expectations

Ask the group leader:

- Why does this group exist?

- What results are expected?

- What will be done with the group's results?

- What is the time frame? Is it realistic?

...Ensure that the right people are involved

Ask the group leader:

- Who has been invited/recruited to this group? Why were they chosen?

- What is each person's position in the organization – department, title, tenure, etc.?

- Which stakeholders who will be affected are not represented in the group?

...Understand the context

Ask the group leader:

- Is there consensus among the organization's leadership about this group's mission?

- Will the larger organization support the group process, the facilitator, and the group's output?

- If needed, will workloads be adjusted so people can focus on their group work?

- What are the available resources within the organization that the group can use?

- What other issues – such as politics, priorities, hidden agendas – are you aware of?

Helping the Group Understand Its Job

Using information you get from the group leader, let the group know:

- Why it was pulled together.

- What results are expected.

- What will be done with the group's results.

- The time frame for getting the job done.

Ideally, the group gets this information in writing and has time to reflect upon it. At your first meeting discuss the information with the group.

Don't move on until everyone in the group is satisfied that they understand exactly what is expected of them.

...Review the process

At the first meeting, give the group an overall picture of how its work will progress over the coming weeks/months. Let participants know that they will be:

- Examining the situation thoroughly and objectively.

- Setting goals and milestones for getting the job done.

- Anticipating and planning for challenges they might face along the way.

- Generating ideas to address those challenges.

- Developing a work plan.

At this point, it's not necessary to talk about techniques. Rather, let the group know how you will guide it through the problem-solving and decision-making efforts. This will:

- Help members understand the benefits of a facilitated approach.

- Gives members the opportunity to ask questions and suggest other approaches.

- Help members understand the role you will be playing vis-à-vis content.

- Create buy-in by reinforcing group ownership of the work.

Defining the Next Steps

The group needs to understand the situation surrounding its job so it can not only figure out what needs to be done and how to do it, but also so it can anticipate and plan for challenges it might face along the way.

...Leave no stone unturned

List the internal and external forces that could have an impact on the group's project—resources, budget, capacity, etc.—and discuss the role each one plays.

List the elements of the situation and generate the questions that arise for each.

List all stakeholders—colleagues, management, city council, the state, customers, employees, sponsor, etc.—and discuss what the interests of each might be.

...Expand, expand

Have the group members list:

- Everything they already know

- What other information they think they need

- Their concerns

- Their hopes

(See Chapter 5 for some approaches for doing this.)

...Identify what's important

Lead the group through sorting and prioritizing those items that they believe will be most important to keep in mind as they move through the process. (See Chapter 5 for ideas on how to do this.) Write these more important items on a flip chart, and post them routinely.

...Set goals and milestones

Now that the group has explored all the facets of the situation surrounding its project, guide participants through describing what needs to happen for their mission to be a success. In addition to developing a vision for the ultimate outcome, have them identify possible hurdles. What will it take to implement the group's vision with each of the stakeholder groups? What will it take to work with the internal and external forces? Have the group list the milestones against which it can measure progress—e.g., developing budgets, procuring supplies, getting approval, soliciting advertising sponsors, raising funds, recruiting volunteers, etc.

...Identify information needs

The group now knows where it is starting from—its situation—and where it wants to end up—its goal. Use the information and ideas the group gathered to determine the next steps.

What If...	*Try...*
...the group leader doesn't have clear expectations?	...meeting with the group leader and asking "What will be different if we succeed? What are you expecting the group to do? How will we know when we are done? What will success look like?"
...the assignment feels unclear to the group?	...restating the desired results. ...explaining the group's role in accomplishing the desired results.
...the group feels stymied by issues beyond its scope?	...asking the team what obstacles are getting in the way of accomplishing objective. ...communicating to the appropriate people outside the group. ...seeking assistance from someone outside the group who has necessary skills or expertise to move ahead.
...the group just wants to get on with the task at hand?	...acknowledging members' task orientation and explaining how the process will help them accomplish their task more effectively and efficiently.
...the group doesn't want ground rules?	...asking the group, "What are your reservations about having ground rules?"
...the group continues to bring up non-relevant issues?	...posting issues in the "parking lot" for all to see, so they will know the issue has been captured and won't be ignored, even though it won't be addressed in *this* discussion.
...the group doesn't like what we're doing or how we're doing it?	...asking the group for ideas on different approaches for achieving its objectives.

Pitfalls to avoid

✔ Allowing the group leader to be ambiguous about why the group exists and the results that are expected. Lack of clarity can compromise the outcome, frustrate group members and result in additional work.

✔ Assuming that everyone understands and agrees with what the group is trying to accomplish. Assumptions can be dangerous!

✔ Confusing activities with results. Starting to work on the "tasks" without agreeing on the desired results can be counterproductive.

✔ Failing to establish checkpoints. Building in milestones ensures keeping the group on track.

CHAPTER 3

PREPARING TO FACILITATE

Topics covered by this chapter

- Why meet?
- Building the agenda.
- Time, location, equipment needs.

Having the Right Frame of Mind

When we asked experienced facilitators to name the challenges new facilitators face, not surprisingly, the most common response was *staying neutral* and *objective about content.*

The second most frequently named challenge? *Fear*, especially when it comes to meetings. It's not uncommon to be nervous about the prospect of facilitating, to worry about the uncertainty and how to help the group focus on the task. The best way to build your confidence is to know that you are prepared.

Why Meet?

Business people say they spend close to 20 hours a week in meetings[1]. That wouldn't be bad, if they didn't also say that a third of the time they spend in meetings is wasted. And people don't really have time to waste; according to a Harris Poll, Americans say they have 20% less leisure time now than they did in 1972[2]. No wonder people pause with dread when a meeting is announced!

How relieved they would be if they knew that this meeting would leave them feeling energized rather than exhausted, affirmed rather than out-shouted, galvanized rather than discouraged! How refreshing it would be if they felt that they could accomplish more in this meeting than they would have accomplished by themselves. How satisfying it would be if they knew that, instead of doing time, they would be making progress. Facilitation can make the difference.

Facilitation is more than meetings. But meetings are still important to group work. It is in meetings that group members come together. The experience of sharing information and ideas, working through problems, and making decisions is most powerful when people are in visual, audio, and physical proximity with one another. So, while facilitation and meeting management aren't synonymous, they are interwoven, and a good facilitator must be good at facilitating meetings, and establishing the appropriate procedures to ensure follow-through on all decisions and action items.

[1] Source: *USA Today*, January 22, 1999.
[2] Source: *American Demographics*, March 2001.

To meet or not to meet?

Don't hold a meeting just because it's scheduled. The only time to have a meeting is when more can be accomplished by getting everyone together at the same time than can be accomplished by other means.

Don't hold a meeting if...

- *Someone only wants to relay information.* Unless he/she is looking for feedback, a memo, letter, or email will probably do just as well.

- *The agenda is relevant to only a few group members.* As much or more can be accomplished through individual discussions or smaller meetings.

- *There are no objectives.* The best way to sentence a group to "doing time" is to call a meeting without clear objectives. Every meeting should seek to have accomplished something by the end of its allotted time period—beyond just having made it to the end of the time period.

Do hold a meeting if the group is looking for...

- Creative solutions

- Agreement on assignments and responsibilities

- New ideas

- Collaborative efforts

- Discussion of important information

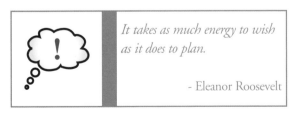

It takes as much energy to wish as it does to plan.

- Eleanor Roosevelt

Why Plan?

To ensure that your meetings make the best use of group members' time, talents, and energies, *plan*. Plan every meeting. Plan, even if you are quick on your feet and confident of your ability to improvise in any situation.

Planning:

- Provides a framework to help the group undertake its mission.

- Lifts the group's confidence in your facilitation skills and its own capabilities.

- Builds the group's momentum and dynamism.

- Motivates group members to attend and participate.

- Encourages group members to come to meetings prepared and to complete tasks between meetings.

- **Makes the difference between a meeting that fails and a meeting that succeeds.**

Balancing planning with flexibility

What if a technique you chose isn't achieving the results for which you hoped? What if someone who was supposed to handle one of the agenda items arrives at the meeting unprepared? What if group members show up for the meeting without having done their prep work? What if the group takes more time on one item than you had budgeted for or finishes earlier than planned? What if your marker runs out of ink?

Having extolled the virtues of preparation, let us now caution against the dangers of rigidity. Don't work yourself into a tizzy worrying about what might go wrong. Just build some flexibility into your plan, which will allow you to:

- Respond positively to requests for revisions to the agenda.

- Be open to the discussion, activity, and energy needs of the group.

- Make changes if the techniques you've chosen aren't working.

- Change direction, if the group needs to.

- Respond to unexpected events with poise and good humor.

The Agenda

A good agenda, distributed to group members before the meeting, helps them prepare, clarifies expectations, and builds interest. During the meeting, it helps keep you and the group focused, and helps you keep track of time and processes.

Prior to each meeting, work with the group leader to prepare the meeting agenda. Determine the purpose and desired outcome for each agenda item.

At the beginning of each meeting, review the agenda with the group and invite suggestions for additions; the group can decide whether the suggestions should be added to the meeting's agenda or "parked" for handling later (either in a future meeting or through some other means).

At the end of each meeting, take suggestions from the group for the next meeting's agenda.

Setting objectives

Work with the group leader to draft objectives for the meeting. Every activity or discussion should result in an outcome—a decision or an action that moves the group's work forward.

Weak Objective	Strong Objective
Discuss the safety situation in plant C	Identify the cause(s) for the increase in the number of accidents in plant C
Ten minutes on funding for the school lunch program	Generate ideas for five sources of funding for the school lunch program
Review options for stimulating volunteerism	Prioritize options for growing volunteerism by 10%

Building the agenda

You can post the agenda on a flip chart at the front of the room or type up something more formal for distribution to each group member prior to the meeting. The agenda can be very detailed or provide just enough information to keep the meeting on track.

Sequence items on the agenda in an order that provides focus for the meeting and makes the most of the group's energy and interest levels.

If you place the most trivial items at the beginning of the meeting, participants might be low on energy by the time they get to the important stuff. If you place the most critical item first, the group might do its "warming up" during the activity, resulting in an unproductive discussion.

If you save the most important items for the end and the meeting runs over, the items won't get the attention and high quality consideration they deserve.

At a minimum, every agenda should include:

- The items to be covered.

- The objective and purpose for each item.

- The amount of time you expect it will take to reach the objective.

The group may also want to know:

- Who in the group is responsible for leading the discussion of each item.

- What techniques will be used for each step.

If you have time to send out the agenda ahead of the meeting, include:

- Meeting time and place.

- List of people attending the meeting, including guests.

- A list of assignments members took on in the previous last meeting.

- A reminder of who promised to bring snacks.

Remember

Include these items on the agenda:

- Check-in
- Review agenda
- Assign meeting roles & responsibilities
- Review/update ground rules as needed

- Break
- Assignments for next meeting
- Next meeting's agenda
- Check-out/evaluation

Meeting Time and Place

Select a date and time based on:

- Group needs
- Project timelines
- Meeting objectives
- Length of agenda
- Organizational priorities
- Schedules of guests
- Availability of meeting space

Select a location based on:

- Number of participants
- Equipment needs
- Ease of access for participants with special needs
- Appropriate seating for discussion and activities
- Wall space for posting note cards and for hanging paper

Pre-meeting materials

To make the most of the time that the group is assembled, try to limit the agenda to those items that are best addressed in a group setting. People might need to get together to ask questions about a report, but probably not to read a report.

Remember...

If you're sending out materials electronically, make sure it's in a format that everyone can access. Do a test run to find out if everyone can open email attachments, and if PC and Mac users can open the attachments they receive from you.

Set come prepared as a ground rule for meetings, and send out materials so that each group member receives them three days prior to the meeting. Information to include:

- The agenda

- Meeting time and place, with driving directions

- A list of people invited to the meeting

- Background reading, including reports and recommendations that will be discussed at the meeting

- A list of assignments members took on in the previous meeting

- Contact information, in case someone has questions, concerns, or can't attend the meeting

Setting Up the Room

Set up the room for meeting success

If...	Then...
...you're planning for a small group discussion	...set up chairs facing each other. Round tables are ideal.
...you're planning for large group discussion	...set up microphones in spots around the room with good sight lines.
...you're planning a "hang-things-on-the-wall" exercise	...make sure there's plenty of wall space, plenty of tacks/tape, and plenty of room for people to move around.
...you're using a board or flip chart	...set it up where everyone can see it.
...some members will participate via teleconference or videoconference	...place the phone/camera/microphone where everyone in the meeting can see/hear, including the people at the other end of the line.

Don't Forget:

- To reserve the space

- To familiarize yourself with the lighting and temperature controls

- To prepare visual aids and handouts

- To pack plenty of supplies: markers, notecards, tape, flip chart paper, newsprint, etc.

- To reserve and test the equipment you'll need

- To order refreshments

Quote

You have to be flexible. If you have a plan and just blindly follow it, it's worse than no plan at all.

- L. F. McCollum

What If...	Try...
...the group has a history of hostility toward facilitators?	...asking the group what they think you will need to know to make their jobs easier and ensure their success. ...asking the group to share hopes and concerns about the project (see Chapter 2).
...I don't know anything about the project the group is going to work on?	...asking the group leader or some knowledgeable person on the team how much you need to know about the content in order to facilitate the process.
...My group rotates facilitation duties? (How much planning do I really need to do?)	...ensuring each facilitator is clear about their role and the processes they will use. ...planning a time to provide feedback from the group to each facilitator.
... I don't have time to plan?	...avoiding the situation at all cost.
...I get to the middle of a meeting and don't know what to do? ...We get to the middle of the meeting and the group doesn't know what to do?	...reading Chapter 4. Discuss with the group and determine how to proceed. ...summarizing the discussion, restating the goals of the group, and discussing options for subsequent activities.
...Materials were sent out in advance, but participants show up unprepared anyway?	...acknowledging the situation and asking the group how they would like to proceed (e.g. taking 15 minutes to read or reschedule).

Pitfalls to avoid

✔ Winging it. Successful facilitation is a result of adequate planning and preparation, which enables the facilitator to focus on the process.

✔ Overplanning. Although planning is important, overplanning may limit the group's flexibility and reduce creativity.

✔ Using tools you don't understand or haven't practiced may result in embarrassment and frustration.

✔ Scheduling a meeting without clear objectives. This most certainly will detract from the group's ability to focus and achieve the desired results.

✔ Having unrealistic expectations about the amount of work people are able or willing to complete. The group's progress may be delayed if members are unable to complete agreed upon tasks and are unprepared for a meeting.

✔ Assuming that the equipment you requested will be there AND will work.

CHAPTER 4

MANAGING MEETINGS

Topics covered by this chapter

■ Facilitator's pre-meeting responsibilities.

■ Methods for effectively opening the meeting.

■ How to create and use Ground Rules to make meetings more productive.

■ Tips and techniques for keeping the meeting moving and focused.

■ Methods for effectively closing the meeting.

Facilitating Meetings

Your responsibilities in facilitating a meeting are to:

- Ensure the room is set up to accommodate the group's needs.

- Open the meeting with a check-in.

- Review the agenda and process.

- Assign meeting tasks.

- Establish or review ground rules.

- Help the group work through the agenda.

- Provide and solicit feedback along the way.

- Plan the next meeting's agenda.

- Close the meeting with a check-out.

Setting Up the Room

Meeting day has arrived! Get there early enough—before the meeting participants—to make sure:

- There are enough chairs and tables.

- The chairs and tables are set up correctly.

- All of your equipment is set up and you know how to use it.

- All of the markers are in good shape.

- There are plenty of notepads, sticky notes, and pens.

- You know where restrooms, phones, etc., are.

Opening the Meeting

Start on time

One of your group's ground rules should be that meetings begin on time. It's a rule that shows respect for everyone's time and sets the tone for a productive meeting that stays on track.

When group members agree to a "begin on time" ground rule, they should also agree on a ground rule for latecomers. Rather than holding up the meeting or rehashing earlier decisions, ask them to meet with you or another group member during a break or after the meeting.

Open with a check-in

A check-in is a very useful introductory activity that can enhance the value of a meeting. The process of asking all participants to "check-in" with the group helps everybody to understand the mood and tone of the participants...where they are "coming from." It also provides the participants an opportunity to let go of their "stuff" so they can be more fully present. The facilitator develops an opening question and asks each group member to respond. The nature and composition of the group will determine the type of question.

Examples of Check-ins

How is everyone feeling?

Share some highlights of your day/week.

Describe your mood as a weather forecast (i.e. sunny, partly cloudy).

What is your most significant accomplishment since we last met?

Tell us about an interesting project you are involved in right now.

Holiday appropriate check-ins. What is your favorite Valentine memory?

Reviewing the Agenda and the Process

Review the agenda with the group, noting who is taking the lead for each item. This is the group's opportunity to ask questions or suggest changes. Resist the temptation to begin discussing any of the agenda items themselves!

Set the stage for the meeting by briefly reviewing the processes and techniques (idea-generation, decision-making by consensus) you'll be using to help the group attain the objectives in the agenda. Use this time to answer questions, not to begin working on the agenda items. **At this point, you're only reviewing the game plan, not playing the game.**

Assigning Responsibilities

Responsibilities that aid facilitation are *recording* and *timekeeping*. Assign them to group members, rather than doing them yourself.

The *recorder* captures ideas, discussion points, and action items on the flip chart or board. This information can be used to create a written document, sometimes known as "minutes." The facilitator can help by:

- Paraphrasing and summarizing what's been said so the words *accurately* capture the intended meaning.

- Identify the key points which should be included in the "minutes." At a minimum they should contain all decisions that were made, future action items, due dates, and the individual responsible for each.

The Power of the Pen

Capturing and writing down ideas as they whiz through the air is a powerful responsibility. The facilitator and recorder need to always make certain that they accurately summarize each idea into a few words. They need to ensure that they aren't inadvertently changing the intended *meaning* of the idea, even if their rewording "sounds better" or "makes more sense." The content of the meeting belongs to the whole group. Note-takers should record information the way it is offered by the participants so that it won't be misinterpreted later on.

Tips for making sure what is written down captures the intended meaning:

- If discussion is moving too rapidly for the recorder, ask people to slow down, back up, or repeat what they've said.

- Ask the recorder to read aloud what they have written down.

- Ask the contributor of the idea if you have captured it the way they would like it captured.

- If an item needs to be shortened, paraphrase it aloud for the group before the recorder writes it down.

- Bring a tape recorder to the meeting. Don't use it in place of note-taking, but as a back-up in case you need to check something later.

- Create a ground rule: One person speaks at a time.

- Create another ground rule: Spelling amnesty.

The *timekeeper* keeps track of time during meetings and lets the group know when the time allocated for discussion of an item is running out. The timekeeper's job is to remind the group of the limits it has set for itself so that adjustments can be made if necessary, and to occasionally ask the group for a "time check." You will need to make sure that the timekeeper's focus on time doesn't drive the meeting.

Participants who take on these responsibilities should be able to do these tasks and still participate fully in the group's activities. If you notice that the timekeeper is so preoccupied with watching the clock that he/she isn't involved in the discussion, give the job to someone else, rotate it around the group, or break it into more "bite-sized" pieces so the group won't lose the benefit of that person's contributions.

Creating Ground Rules

Creating ground rules should be a primary objective for your group's first meeting. At subsequent meetings, review the ground rules at the same time that you review the agenda and meeting processes.

The group's best protection against being derailed by unproductive behavior is through agreeing on expectations at the *beginning* of the process for how group members will work together, actively making decisions, assigning work, and handling disagreements as they arise. One of the most effective ways to facilitate the formation of ground rules is to present one of the areas (e.g. attendance) and ask the group to suggest specific rules for each area.

The group also needs to agree upon how the ground rules will be used and what happens when they are not followed. For example, if the group decides to always start meetings on time, what will happen if someone comes late? What will be the group's response if members don't come prepared to meetings or follow up on assignments?

The facilitator should participate in the framing of ground rules, but he/she should resist the urge to take responsibility for enforcement. **The ground rules belong to the group and need to be monitored by the group.** The agreed upon ground rules should be posted and visible to all group members.

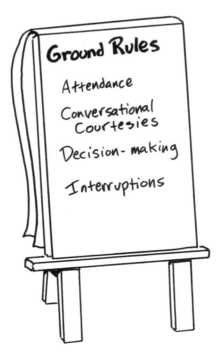

Ground Rules to Consider

Attendance What are the expectations for attendance?	*Sample ground rules:* • A member who is going to miss a meeting should contact James 24 hours in advance. • The minimum number of meetings that everybody attends is… • Three-quarters of the group must be present in order to hold a meeting.
Promptness	*Sample ground rules:* • Meetings start and end on time. • Latecomers and early-leavers are responsible for catching up on what they missed without disrupting the meeting.
Conversational courtesies How will the group manage itself while exchanging ideas?	*Sample ground rules:* • One person speaks at a time. • No personal comments or sarcasm. • All ideas will be listened to respectfully. • Don't "filibuster the airspace" (45 second rule). • Check your title at the door. • No side conversations.
Interruptions How will the group respond to beeping pagers, ringing cell phones, and knocks on the door during meetings?	*Sample ground rules:* • Pagers and cell phones will be turned off during meetings.

Ground Rules to Consider

Confidentiality

How will the group treat information that is proprietary, dangerous, painful, or embarrassing?

Sample ground rules:

- Personal information shared during a meeting does not leave the room.
- A member who wishes to share information with someone outside the group must clear it with the group first.
- Group members will apprise one another of discussions they have outside of meetings to keep everyone in the loop.

Routine tasks

How will the group take responsibility for note-taking, report-writing, time-keeping, room-reserving, donut-bringing…?

Sample ground rules:

- Everyone in the group will take a turn doing each job.
- If someone is not able to do his/her job, he/she will find a substitute.

Decision-making

How will decisions be made?

Sample ground rules:

- Decisions will be made by consensus.
- Highest-ranking members speak last.

Preparedness

How should participants prepare themselves for a meeting?

Sample ground rules:

- Read preparation materials before the meeting.
- Preparation materials will be distributed three days before each meeting.

Assignments

What are the expectations for tasks which need to be completed outside scheduled meeting times?

Sample ground rules:

- Complete assignments between meetings.
- No assignment should be so big that it can't be completed before the next meeting.

Ground Rules to Consider

New members	Sample ground rules:
How will new members be assimilated into the group?	• Group leader will bring new members up to speed before their first meeting. • Build a getting-to-know-you check-in to the new members' first meeting.
Ground rule effectiveness How will the group review the effectiveness of the ground rules?	*Sample ground rules:* • The whole group takes responsibility for following and enforcing ground rules. • Ground rules will be reviewed at the start of every meeting and revised as the group sees appropriate. • Anyone who breaks the same ground rule three times in one meeting has to bring the donuts for the next meeting but doesn't get to eat any of them.

Working together to develop ground rules requires members to articulate their values and set norms for ways of communicating and working with one another. The members begin to feel like a group because the rules came from them, not from the organization, the group leader, or the facilitator. The group becomes more cohesive as individuals take responsibility for upholding their rules with one another.

Keeping the Group Focused and Moving Forward

Because one of the things groups do is meet, an important aspect of the facilitator's job is helping members work together in meetings. A meeting that keeps moving and stays focused is a meeting that is productive, effective, and fun. Keep yours on track by...

...Observing

- "There seems to be concern about…"
- "Perhaps it's time to move on…"
- "Is this something we should continue next week, when…?"

...Clarifying

- "What I hear you saying is…"
- "Let's see if we can clear up the confusion…"
- "If I understand correctly…"
- "Is there anything about this that is still unclear?"
- "Let's review where we are…"

...Focusing

- "Getting back to the agenda…"
- "Can we park this issue for now and get back to the topic we've been discussing?"
- "Let's get back to our flip chart…"
- "The point currently under discussion is…"

...Stimulating

- "What ideas can we come up with…?"
- "How could we approach this question from a different angle?"
- "What might be other reasons for this situation?"
- "Is this a good place to do some idea generation?"
- "What do you think about…?"
- "For example, has anyone ever…?"

...Balancing

- "Does anyone else have another viewpoint?"
- "Any other ideas?"
- "Beth, what else do you think might work?"

...Summarizing

- "To review the key points we've heard today…"

- "Let's look again at the decisions we've made…"

- "Before we move to the next item let's record the key points from the discussion…"

- "In summary, we are going to…"

- "Sam will follow up on…"

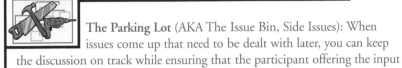

HOW TO | *Deal With Issues: The Parking Lot*

The Parking Lot (AKA The Issue Bin, Side Issues): When issues come up that need to be dealt with later, you can keep the discussion on track while ensuring that the participant offering the input gets heard and his/her input doesn't get lost.

Hang a sheet of paper on the wall and call it *The Parking Lot*. Park side issues there until the end of the meeting. The recorder can jot them down as they arise or participants can write them on sticky notes you've placed around the table. Ask the group how it wants to work with the issues that haven't yet been addressed, for example, by adding them to the next meeting agenda or assigning them to the appropriate person to tackle.

Managing the agenda

Handle one item at a time. Introduce the item and the person responsible for bringing that item to the group. Review the objective for the item.

Maintain focus throughout the meeting. Stick to the agenda. Create a "parking lot" to capture items that come up and deserve attention some other time.

Facilitate the process for achieving the objective for each item before moving on. If the objective has been achieved, clarify agreements, next steps, and individual group members' responsibilities for next steps. If the group is going to need more time to achieve the objective, help it identify what further work needs to be done, and decide whether that work will be done in this meeting—in which case the agenda needs to be adjusted—or put it on the agenda for the next meeting.

Summarize agreements and test for consensus before moving on to the next item.

Making decisions

A common mistake that groups make is thinking that, because they have come to the end of the time allotted for an agenda item, they have done their job. When a group "does time" instead of doing work, it runs the risk of having unresolved agenda items come up again and again. If you've ever felt that your group has the same meeting over and over again, it's probably because it hasn't made the decisions it needs to. If your group is unable to complete a decision-making process in the session, make a note of where you are in the process and **save the flip charts.**

For information on decision-making methods, see Chapter 5.

Providing and soliciting feedback

The group needs your help staying focused, on track, and productive. Because you are committed to remaining neutral regarding the content of its discussions, you are in a good position to observe and provide feedback regarding how the group is doing.

This is tricky business. Sometimes people hear fault-finding where none is intended. The most innocent clarifying question can be misinterpreted as a confrontation, especially when discussing a topic one feels strongly about.

The key to providing constructive feedback is to focus on those behaviors that are helping the group move toward its goals – and those that are slowing it down. This means offering both affirming and critical feedback. It means talking about specific behavior, not personalities.

It definitely does not mean reading into someone's behavior what you think his/her motives, attitudes, or psychological profile might be. Don't make sweeping general statements: "You always…" or "You never…" Don't be judgmental or use labels.

Do

- Be specific: "These cell phone calls are distracting to our discussion."

- Use constructive feedback = descriptive + prescriptive (describe what is happening AND how to improve it)

- Be kind: If feedback would embarrass someone in front of the group, provide it privately during a break.

- Invite people to offer suggestions: "How can we reduce the interruptions to our meeting?"

- Let people know what they can do to help the meeting run more effectively: "Minimizing distractions will help us have a more productive meeting."

- Show appreciation for behavior that helps move the group's work forward. "Thank you for turning off your cell phone when you came into the meeting."

Review decisions and action items

Before you close the meeting, make sure that the recorder has accurately captured all of the decisions the group has made. These include the next steps, who will be responsible for them, and the date by which tasks will be completed. List these on the flip chart *and* in the meeting minutes.

Closing the Meeting

Planning the next agenda

Review the decisions of the group to ensure that everyone is clear about what actions are being taken and by whom. Make a list of items participants think should be on the next meeting's agenda, the objectives and the name of the person responsible for taking the lead on each one. Use this list when you work with the group leader to plan the next meeting.

Check-out

Briefly go around the room and ask for input regarding how the meeting went. What were some notable accomplishments today? Where did we struggle? What were the highlights of today's meeting? What should we do differently next time? Use this feedback to help you plan for the next meeting.

TIPS FOR *Teleconference Meetings*

- Build the agenda *before* the meeting.

- Be sure all participants are aware of any time zone differences.

- Make sure everyone gets a copy of the agenda ahead of time.

- Have all materials labeled and identified by different colors.

- Make sure phone and video equipment are working.

- Plan processes that don't require physical cues or interaction, such as round robin discussions, rather than idea generation.

- Establish "one at a time" as a ground rule for discussion, making sure people wait to comment on a topic until the speaker is finished.

- Call on each participant by name.

- Ask participants to identify themselves before speaking.

- Periodically update the person(s) on the phone as to what's going on in the room. This is particularly helpful when there is silence.

- Rein in ambient noises, such as crumbling paper, clattering dishes, side conversations, pencils tapping on the table, etc.

- Plan for a "bio break" if the call exceeds $1^1/_2$–2 hrs. Be clear about the length of break and the procedure for reconnecting the call.

- Use humor. Tell people what you are not seeing is Jack scratching his head or Tom staring into space.

Reasons I love teleconferencing...

1) I can wear my favorite sweats and sit in my easy chair.

2) No one knows if I am having a bad hair day.

3) My facial expressions don't have to be censored.

4) (Put your favorite reason here...)

What If...	Try...
...a key decision-maker is late or absent?	...asking the group if this person's absence/tardiness hinders the group's process. If the answer is yes, agree to reschedule or delay the meeting. ...seeing if there is a way you can reorder the agenda to take this into consideration.
...someone comes in late and wants to be caught up?	...offering to brief the latecomer during the break. ...providing a brief explanation as to where the group is with the agenda. ...establishing a ground rule that addresses the issue for future meetings.
...our group seems too large for a check-in?	...asking an open-ended question and inviting people to respond to it. Give the group an appropriate amount of time to answer (not everyone is required to respond).
...group members want to change course once the meeting starts?	...asking, "What has changed since we put this plan in place?" and adapt, if appropriate.
...participants object to the process or parts of it.	...asking the others if they share this concern. If so, ask the group for alternative approaches.
...the group wants *me* to take a participant role?	...determining why the group feels it is important for you to participate. Discuss your concerns about doing both.
...The group is engaged in a meaningful discussion but time is running out?	...bringing the situation to the group's attention by sharing your perception ("this is a very meaningful discussion") and discuss how to proceed—extend the meeting? schedule additional time? reconfigure the agenda? etc.

What If...	Try...
...the group expects *me* to enforce the ground rules?	...reminding the group that the ground rules are the *group's* rules, so are a shared responsibility. ... checking with the group regarding whether the ground rules they don't want to enforce should be removed from their list.
...one person consistently breaks the ground rules?	...meeting with the individual outside the meeting, providing feedback about the effect his/her behavior is having on the group's effectiveness, and asking for cooperation.
...the group leader dominates discussion, tries to control decisions, or won't follow the same rules as everyone else?	...meeting with the individual outside the meeting, providing feedback about the effect his/her behavior is having on the group's effectiveness, and asking for cooperation.
...I suddenly realize I don't have enough time to get through the agenda?	...asking the group, "What should we focus on for the rest of the meeting?" ...determining, "How should the remaining items be addressed?" ...asking for volunteers to work outside the meeting on agenda items the group didn't have time to cover in this meeting.
...the group members are uncomfortable with giving and receiving feedback.	...using a variety of questions: "What went well?" "Where did we struggle?" "Next time we should..."
...I am uncomfortable with how things are going?	...sharing your views with the group. Check if members feel the same way. (Your discomfort with the process may not be shared by the group.)

Pitfalls to avoid

✔ Underestimating the importance of introductory activities (check-in, ground rules, etc.). These activities help participants get comfortable and get the meeting off to a productive start.

✔ Not allowing enough "prep" time to ensure that the facilities and equipment are working properly.

✔ Abusing the "power of the pen" by not accurately recording what is discussed.

✔ Neglecting to agree in advance on how decision-making will happen.

✔ Assuming things are going well if nobody is complaining. No news is NOT necessarily good news to a facilitator.

✔ Getting so involved in the meeting content that you do not observe how the group is working.

CHAPTER 5

IDEA GENERATION

Topics covered by this chapter

The facilitator's role in helping the group:

■ Generate ideas.

■ Sort and categorize ideas.

■ Prioritize and select ideas.

Generating and Sorting Ideas

I never did anything by accident, nor did any of my inventions come by accident; they came by work...Genius is ninety-nine percent perspiration and one percent inspiration.

-Thomas A. Edison

While some may think of creativity as a gift for producing a painting, melody, or poem, creativity is nothing more than the ability to imagine. Every child who has figured out how to reach the cookie jar atop the refrigerator, every parent who has figured out how to fit orthodontics into a tight budget, and every person who has figured out how to transform a cubicle into a friendly space with a few family photos has demonstrated an ability for creating solutions to problems.

Group idea generation is rich in rewards because of the diversity of perspectives members bring to the process. Cast the net deep and wide, and participants will find themselves breaking free from old thinking patterns as ideas trigger new ideas. A well-facilitated idea-generation session will allow group members to generate ideas as fast as the recorder can write them down. The more ideas generated, the greater the likelihood that the group will find good ones to work with.

Guidelines for idea generation

Because the group is, first, striving to generate as many ideas as it can, you'll want to suggest these proven ground rules that will encourage free and open expression of ideas and keep the ideas flowing.

Some possible ground rules:

- No criticism or judgment of ideas until after the idea-generation exercise is finished.

- All ideas are worthwhile and encouraged.

- Building on others' ideas is a good idea.

- All ideas should be written on the board with no comment.

- Each person has up to 30 seconds to describe an idea.

Behaviors that inhibit the flow and expression of ideas include:

- Pausing to discuss each idea.

- Commenting on ideas.

- Criticizing or judging ideas.

- Over-controlling by the facilitator or a dominating group member.

Tools for idea generation

Idea-generation meetings can be either free-wheeling or structured. This chapter describes tools for generating and sorting ideas. The process of generating ideas is usually more effective if groups don't always rely on the same idea-generation technique—using a variety of tools gives members the opportunity to look at situations from a variety of angles. The tool you choose should take into account the objective and the type of situation being addressed.

Stimulating Creativity

- Ask group members for their wildest ideas. Make sure that each one gets voiced and recorded.

- Give the group a visual stimulus. Show pictures, slides, posters, or objects; they don't need to be related to the situation being discussed.

- Ask group members to role play, to think about the situation from a different perspective. "What kind of ideas would a customer come up with?", " The CFO?", "How would a newscaster report the situation?"

- Give the group an audio stimulus to get the right side of the brain working. Play any kind of music, loud or soft, classical or contemporary, rock or country, blues or jazz.

- Invite group members to keep notes on ideas they get between meetings. Have them ask non-group members for ideas. Ask for reports at the next meeting.

- Provide art supplies and ask the group to create a visual.

Brainstorming

Brainstorming asks participants to express their ideas out loud, listing every idea they can think of. Sharing thoughts in this way stimulates the thinking of other group members and can result in a list of ideas both expansive and ingenious. There are two alternatives for accomplishing this: 1) members contribute ideas as they come to mind, or 2) if more structure is needed, go around the room with members contributing ideas one at a time. The result is a long list of ideas, some far-fetched, some brilliant, some both.

Brainstorming sessions are characterized by waves of high energy and free-wheeling participation punctuated by periods of silence. Don't be afraid of lulls – they mark the beginning of a new wave and often yield even more creative ideas.

Remember...

- Review the ground rules for brainstorming.
- Use verbal cues. ("What else?" "Say more.")
- Encourage contributions and thank participants.
- Post responses. Keep all ideas in front of the group.
- Avoid making comments, good or bad, during idea generation.
- Check for clarity and common understanding by paraphrasing when necessary.
- Do not contribute ideas. Your job is to manage the process.
- Remember the power of the pen.

HOW TO | *Generate Ideas: Brainstorming*

Prior to the brainstorming session: Develop a statement of the problem and give advanced notice that the team will be brainstorming for possible solutions to the problem.

During the Session:

1) Begin the meeting with a review of brainstorming and establish the four rules of brainstorming.

   The Ground Rules:
   a. Criticism or judgment of ideas is deferred until after idea generation.

   b. Free-wheeling is welcomed. All ideas are worthwhile and encouraged.

   c. Quantity is desired. The more ideas generated, the greater the odds that a successful solution will be found.

   d. Combination and improvement on the ideas of others is a good practice. It can produce more creative ideas.

2) Write the problem statement on a board or a flip chart that is visible to everyone on the team.

3) You will usually act as "recorder" to write down all the ideas generated. Use the flip chart. A second recorder may be helpful.

4) Set an approximate time frame for idea generation. Usually 15–30 minutes works best in team meetings.

Tip: If the issue is complex or challenging in some way, it might work best if you give the team members 5 minutes to write down their ideas individually before beginning the open session.

5) Continue brainstorming for the allotted time. Don't be afraid of lulls. Often a team will get more creative after a lull. Don't end the brainstorming prematurely.

Tip: To increase the energy level, encourage people to move around.

Adaptation: Try a "round-robin" recording of ideas instead of a free-wheeling session. In a round-robin session, you go around the table seeking ideas from one person at a time. Continue around until there are no ideas left. Team members can pass if they can't think of something when it's their turn. Be certain to enforce a "no-speaking-out-of-turn" rule. The round-robin is more structured and can lead to a more balanced participation by reducing the prospects for domination by a few people.

Brainwriting

When you eliminate verbal discussion, you also eliminate the negative consequences which can accompany group discussions. Brainwriting assures anonymity and eliminates interaction with other individuals. In addition, it accommodates and incorporates those individuals who need time to reflect on their ideas.

This method of writing ideas on paper is likely to produce innovative ideas. The main weakness is that there may be some loss of spontaneity because the ideas are collected silently and without group interaction. If more diversity in idea content is desired, additional stimuli or aids (pictures, sounds, etc.) can be used.

HOW TO   *Generate Ideas: Brainwriting*

1) Review the process and the ground rules with the team.

The Ground Rules:
a. Work silently.
b. All ideas are worthwhile and valuable.
c. Write legibly so others can read what you have to say.
d. Keep it moving. Don't get stuck on one thought.

2) Present the problem statement to the team.

3) The team members write down their ideas on a sheet of paper.

4) As soon as an individual has listed an idea, place the sheet in the middle of the table and exchange it for another sheet. Call it the "Idea Pool."

5) Participants continue to add one idea to the sheets taken from the pool, exchanging them for a new sheet after each additional idea. A team member can use the same sheet more than once. Members can build on the ideas already on the sheet or add entirely new thoughts.

6) Set an approximate time frame for idea generation. Usually 15–30 minutes works best in team meetings.

7) Collect the sheets and consolidate all the ideas into one document or onto a flip chart. Once this is done, the team can begin to evaluate the ideas.

Affinity process

The affinity process is a tool for generating and categorizing related issues or themes. The process involves verbal and non-verbal steps. It combines idea generation and the beginning of decision-making because the team has to agree on the organization of ideas. This process can also be used to organize comments or complaints from customers, to collect ideas from non-group members, or to identify causes of a problem.

Affinity sessions are dynamic and fun. The process works best when participants provide ideas that are clear and unambiguous.

HOW TO   *Generate and Sorting Ideas: Affinity Process*

1) Phrase the issue or question clearly to the team. Establish the ground rules.

The Ground Rules:

a. Part of the session will be done in silence.

b. No one-word cards. No clichés.

c. Avoid ambiguous words or phrases.

2) Ask the team members to write their ideas on large (4″ x 6″) note cards or Post-it™ Notes. Ask them to print in clear, large letters using felt tip pens.

3) Ask participants to put their Post-its™ on the wall or lay their cards on the table randomly.

4) Ask team members to *silently* sort the cards or Post-its™ into what they see as related groupings. Anyone may regroup a card if he/she feels it is in the wrong category. *Tip:* If one card keeps getting moved around, write a duplicate card so that the idea can be in two places. It's okay if some cards stand alone. End this step when the team seems to be settled on most of the groupings. This usually takes about ten minutes.

5) Begin the discussion of the groupings with the team.
   A. Sort any ungrouped cards through discussion.
   B. Consolidate duplicate cards.
   C. Identify a theme for each grouping.

6) Create header cards for each group. Keep the number of headers in the range of 5–15 groups.

7) If any single grouping seems much larger than the others, have the team divide it into sub-headings.

Decision-Making

Our company has, indeed, stumbled onto some of its new products. But never forget that you can't stumble if you're not moving.

-Richard P. Carleton
former CEO, 3M

Once group members have grappled with the framing question and generated multiple ideas for how to approach the situation, they are ready to prioritize and select ideas

Consensus-building

While there are a number of ways to arrive at decisions—voting, lottery, dictum—the more effective groups make their decisions through consensus.

When a group reaches consensus, it has agreed on a decision that every person "can live with." This means that everyone in the group has agreed to support the decision, even if some members might have wished for a slightly different decision. Consensus-building is a process, a way of approaching information-gathering, idea-generating, and decision-making that moves the group toward its most effective outcome.

When a decision is reached by consensus, each group member should be able to honestly say:

- "I believe the group understands my point of view."

- "I believe I understand the points of view in the group."

- "This might not have been my first choice, but I can live with it."

- "I will support this decision because it was reached in an open and fair manner."

Consensus-building is an expression of trust, respect for one another and a commitment to the group's mission. While other approaches to decision-making, such as voting, may seem faster, consensus speeds implementation because a decision reached by consensus has gained the buy-in of the entire group. Whenever possible, use consensus-building to optimize communication, motivate group members to work together on implementation, and minimize the risk of sabotage by disgruntled members.

HOW TO | *Make Decisions:* Consensus-Building

- Summarize the team's work up to this point. Clarify the issue and review the options.

- Identify points of agreement.

- Identify points of disagreement.

- Listen carefully to everyone's point of view and rationale.

- Make sure the team sticks to the Ground Rules during all discussions.

- Determine the underlying assumptions and discuss the validity of those assumptions.

- Obtain additional data, if necessary, to validate those assumptions.

- Use techniques and tools, such as multi-voting and decision matrix, to help the team develop the best solution.

Tools for decision-making

The time for freewheeling has come to an end. Decision-making calls for a structured review of all the ideas on the table and a sifting through of the ones that look most promising. This chapter describes two techniques for helping the group decide which ideas they want to work with: multi-voting and decision matrix. The tool you choose should take into account the group's size and dynamics, the type of situation being examined, and the number and nature of the ideas that have been generated.

Multi-voting

Multi-voting is a way to select the most important or popular items from a list with a minimum amount of discussion. It's a good technique for paring down a long list of ideas into a shorter list for in-depth discussion. Even a large list of fifty items can be reduced to a workable number later.

Don't use multi-voting as a tool for making final decisions; it's a good tool for stimulating discussion, but not for achieving consensus.

HOW TO — *Prioritize and Select Ideas:* Multi-Voting

1) After brainstorming, brainwriting or other creative idea generation techniques, list the potential solutions on a flip chart or board.

2) Number each item.

3) Have the team review the list. If two or more items seem very similar, combine them, but only if the team agrees that they are the same. Don't let the team get bogged down in this exercise. If it is not clear that items can be combined, leave them alone and proceed with the vote.

4) Have the team members "vote" for several items by writing down the numbers of these items on a sheet of paper in front of them. Each team member is allowed to vote for items equal to at least one-third of the total number of items on the list. (60-item list = 20 choices, 38-item list = 13 choices, etc.)

5) Tally the votes. This can be done by:

   a. Allowing team members to come up and mark their votes next to the items using checks or hash marks. (This is also a way to get people moving in the meeting).

   b. Asking for a show of hands as you go through the list.

   c. Collecting ballots and recording the votes during a break or between sessions thus ensuring anonymity, if necessary.

6) Cross out the items receiving the fewest number of votes. Don't try to reduce the list in one round if you have more than 15 items.

7) Repeat steps 4–6 with the remaining items on the list. Remember to readjust the number of votes allowed each team member to one-third of the items remaining on the list.

8) Continue this process until a manageable number, 7 or fewer items, remain.

9) Have the team discuss the remaining items. Switch to a decision matrix technique to achieve a final decision.

Remember...

The group needs to stick to its ground rules in all discussions.

Decision matrix

The perfect choice rarely exists. Options A and B (but not C) might meet some criteria, while A and C (but not B) meet another set of criteria. D might meet some critical criteria but be lacking in every other area. The boss might prefer E for no other reason than that it's his wife's favorite color. The decision matrix helps teams objectively evaluate alternative options and is particularly useful if the situation is complex with many interwoven variables.

A commonly applied adaptation is to assign ranking or weighting to both the options and the criteria against which the options should be measured. Through this technique, the group gains an understanding of not only the efficacy of each option, but also the relative importance of each criteria used to evaluate its options. Caution: While decision matrix can be an objective method for decision-making, it may not lend itself to issues that are highly qualitative.

HOW TO  ***Prioritize and Select Ideas:*** *Decision Matrix*

1) Draw a matrix on a flip chart.

2) List the options/ideas in any order down the left side of the matrix.

3) Across the top, list the criteria for evaluation. *Option:* Ask the team to assign a weight to each criterion that reflects its relative importance. For example: 1 = low importance, 2 = moderate importance, etc.

4) Rate each option/idea against the criteria. Use a 0–5 point scale, e.g., 5 = completely meets criterion, 0 = does not meet criterion at all. Determine ratings by team consensus.

5) Multiply the rating by the weighted score. Write the number in the corresponding box in the matrix.

6) Add up the weighted ratings and write the total in the final right-hand column headed "Total Weighted Rating."

7) Discuss the high-ranking ideas to reach consensus on which is the best solution. The matrix is a tool that helps build consensus. Don't automatically adopt the highest score. Discuss the high-ranking alternatives.

Quick-Check-Why

This process provides a group the opportunity to hear and express opinions on different options that have been identified. Created by Liz Freeman and Roland Coates, Quick-Check-Why is particularly effective when there are a number of variables, criteria and less tangible issues. By following a structured process, the important issues emerge in an atmosphere of openness and respect. Although primarily designed to help a group reach consensus, this process can also be used to help a group clarify issues. Post the rules (number 1-5 below) for the Quick-Check-Why process in a conspicuous place at the meeting.

Quick-Check-Why

1) List all options or identified possibilities so that they are visible to all.

2) A round of "quick checks" to learn the current situation.

   a. One person at a time, everyone is asked to "state your preferred choice at this point in time." During this round, no reasons are to be offered and no discussion takes place.

   b. The facilitator puts a hash mark by the choices that are indicated.

This round provides an opportunity for the group to see where everyone stands. It could be that everyone has the same choice. Listening to each other also helps to release the tension caused by wanting to know where others stand.

3) A round of reasons to understand the "why."

   a. One person at a time, everyone explains why they have chosen what they have chosen. They may also state what they don't like about the other possibilities. This is the only time when they may argue against another position.

   b. As everyone presents their reasons, all are asked to LISTEN and be open to the possibilities.

   c. It's okay to ask questions for clarification, but judgments are not allowed. Save rebuttals for your turn.

Continued on next page

Quick-Check-Why (continued)

During clarification, there is a tendency to try to "disguise" a rebuttal as a question. ("You don't mean . . . do you?" or "Yes, but don't you think that . . ."). If it takes longer to ask a question than the original description, it is likely NOT a question for clarification.

When this happens, the facilitator can ask the group "Does that sound like a clarification question?"

4) Another round of "quick checks."

    a. One person at a time, everyone is asked "At this point in time, where do you stand?"

    b. Go in order, starting with the next person in the round. No reasons are to be offered and no discussion takes place. This round provides opportunity for the group to see if there has been any movement towards consensus.

5) Repeat rounds of "why" followed by rounds of "quick checks."

    a. Continue until consensus is reached.

    b. Ask members to be willing to modify their views.

    c. Members are encouraged to pass if they have no additional perspectives.

What If...	Try...
...the group is stuck on a few ideas?	...using methods for "stimulating" more ideas, as described on pages 52–57.
...the group is reluctant to use the techniques I selected?	...asking the group, "What are your reservations about using this technique?" and adjust accordingly. ...checking your own assumptions about the technique you chose for accomplishing the stated objective.
...the idea selected exceeds the scope or authority of the group?	...checking that it IS outside the scope. ...informing the group, "This idea seems to be outside the scope of this group...what is the most appropriate next step?"
...everyone defers to a few key people?	...sharing your observation with the group. "I have noticed a trend which I want to discuss with you." "It appears to me that the group is deferring most of the decisions to a few people." Pause and allow people time to respond.
...the group can't agree on an issue?	...asking the group, "What is preventing us from moving forward?" ...using multi-voting or the decision matrix to help the group.

Pitfalls to avoid

✔ Jumping to solutions too quickly. It is important for the group to explore all aspects of the issue prior to moving to solutions.

✔ Taking too much responsibility for the decisions that are made. This can compromise the group's ownership of the decision they have made.

✔ Not using the guidelines for idea generation. Guidelines ensure the integrity of the process and if not used effectively, they can have a negative impact on the quality and number of ideas that are generated.

✔ Using brainstorming for decision-making. Brainstorming is a tool for idea generation. Do not allow the group to act on an idea without further consideration.

✔ Reacting to ideas being offered. Effective brainstorming requires the facilitator to remain neutral and not comment on the ideas generated.

✔ Overemphasis on one tool. Depending on the task, and the length of the project, it is important to use a variety of tools, which may provide the group with alternative methods of approaching the same problem.

CHAPTER 6

PLANNING & IMPLEMENTATION

Topics covered by this chapter

The facilitator's role in helping the group:

■ Planning the next steps.

■ Identifying time frames and resource needs.

■ Determining responsibilities.

Next Steps

The Facilitator's Role

Questions have been raised and addressed. Information has been gathered and examined. Ideas have been generated and sorted. The group has made the tough decisions regarding priorities. What to do with all this good stuff?

Regardless of whether the group was convened to formulate a plan, or to develop recommendations for a plan that will be implemented by someone else, it's time to organize what it has learned into a roadmap for action. The facilitator's role is to guide the group through:

- Setting objectives.
- Determining steps for achieving the objectives.
- Setting time frames for each step.
- Identifying resource needs.
- Establishing responsibility.

What needs to be accomplished? When everything is said and done, where will we be and what will be different? How will we know when we have succeeded?

Your group has probably already figured out the answers, based on the work it has done.

Work with the group to state the objective in one sentence:

- "Develop a logo that effectively differentiates our product from the competition."
- "Raise $40,000 for a new playground."
- "Increase the use of e learning in our business by 25%."

The objective should be *specific, actionable,* and *measurable.*

Determining the Next Steps

What needs to take place in order for the objective to be achieved? In what sequence should events occur? How can all of the information and decision points be managed effectively?

Here are some tools to guide your group through the process.

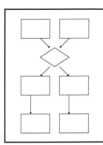

Flowchart

A flowchart is a graphic representation of a process. It can be used to show where things happen in a project and/or how they're dependent upon and connected to one another. It's also a good way to discover complexities and redundancies that perhaps weren't noticed before.

HOW TO | **Determine Steps:** *Flowchart*

- Use the plan objective as the starting point.

- List all the actions that need to happen in order to achieve the objective, including resources that need to be called upon and decisions that need to be made. Put each event on an index card or sticky note, so you can shift them around easily.

- Arrange the actions on a table in the order they need to happen. If two things need to happen simultaneously, place them side-by-side. If action A needs to happen before event B can happen, place action B underneath action A.

- Resolve the loops, redundancies, and over-complications.

- On a large sheet of paper, make a box for each action, and draw all the boxes in the same order you've arranged them on the table.

  - Use a rectangle to show a task or an action.

  - Use a diamond to show a yes/no decision point.

  - Use an oval to show the starting and finishing points of the process.

- Draw arrows to indicate the flow of events.

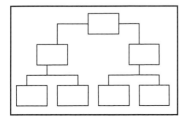

Tree Diagram

The tree diagram is a good way to organize steps that grow increasingly complex, by breaking them down to bite-sized pieces.

HOW TO — *Determine Steps: Tree Diagram*

- Use the plan objective for the tree diagram goal statement. Write this on an index card or sticky note.

- Generate sub goals, using the headers from an affinity process or another sorting exercise the group has done. These are the strategies or means that will be used to reach the objective. Write these down and place them under the objective statement.

- Break each of these into actions. These are the tactics that will be used to implement the strategies.

- Break each of these into greater detail.

- When the group is satisfied that it has broken the work into manageable pieces, capture the chart on a large piece of paper.

Contingency Planning

What if something goes wrong? What if something delays or accelerates the schedule? How will the organization respond to problems with the implementation plan? Should the group propose a back-up plan? Are there any safety valves built into the plan?

If the group is writing a plan they will implement or, which will be implemented by someone else, it is a good idea to anticipate potential obstacles and have a Plan B. The troll search, force field analysis, and contingency diagram are three tools for avoiding potential problems.

Troll search

Trolls are the fears and obstacles that emerge from "under the bridge" to derail a project. They can come from outside or within the group. It is a good idea to conduct a troll search several times over the life of a project to reduce the chance of trolls rearing their heads at awkward moments in the process.

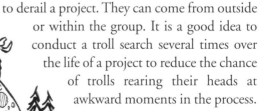

HOW TO | *Anticipate Problems: Troll Search*

- Brainstorm everything that could go wrong.

- For each item, calculate both the likelihood of it happening and the severity of its occurrence, on a 0-10 scale.

• Assign each "troll" to a smaller group or to individuals within larger groups. These group members will be responsible for keeping an eye on their "trolls," i.e., to develop contingency plans and implement them should the "troll" emerge for real.

• Periodically review the "trolls" to see which ones have been eliminated, which ones still need attention, and whether any new ones have been born.

Force field analysis

The force field reveals what forces might be working for or against an action. By presenting positives and negatives for easy comparison, this tool can help people anticipate and address potential implementation problems.

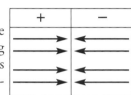

HOW TO | *Anticipate Problems: Force Field Analysis*

- Write the strategy or tactic you want to analyze.

- Underneath it, draw a large "T". Mark one side with a "+" and the other with a "-".

• On the "+" side, list all the reasons the strategy will succeed (driving forces). On the "-" side, list all the hurdles or obstacles it might encounter (restraining forces).

• Once the group has identified all the driving forces and restraining forces, you can help them identify ways to strengthen the driving forces and deal with the restraining ones.

Example: Improving Customer Service

Driving Forces (+)	→ ←	Restraining Forces (-)
Empower employees in decision-making		Lack of knowledge/skills by our CSRs
Have measurement systems in place		Don't have shared understanding of LCS
Learn about customer-satisfaction level		Don't know enough about our customers
Our customers are loyal to us	→ ←	Lack urgency re: value of our customers

Contingency diagram

A contingency diagram can help the group analyze and counteract forces working against its plan.

HOW TO   *Contingency Plan: Contingency Diagram*

- Following a force field analysis, select the restraining forces that seem most difficult to overcome.
- List all the events that might happen that would bring about the undesired state.
- Beside each event on the list, brainstorm the actions the group might take to prevent it from happening. Sort and select the ones that seem the most effective and efficient.
- Write these steps into the plan.

Identifying Resource Needs

What resources will it take to implement the plan? For each step, identify what will be needed in terms of...

- Money
- People
- Time
- Space
- Equipment

What if one or more of these resources isn't as available as you'd like? Are there alternatives?

Plan ahead. It wasn't raining when Noah built the Ark.

-Richard Cushing

Establishing Responsibility

Who in the group will do what? If the plan is being built for someone outside the group to implement, what roles need to be filled?

Matrix

A matrix diagram can be used to identify what needs to be done and who needs to do it. It provides an easy way to visually check that tasks are distributed appropriately among group members.

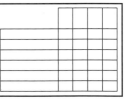

HOW TO   *Distribute Tasks: Decision Matrix*

• Create columns and rows on a flip chart.

• In each column, write the name of a role (e.g., production manager, art department, sales manager) or the names of the individuals who will be implementing the plan.

• In each row, write a task.

• Identify who will have primary responsibility for each task with a "☆."

• Identify who needs to be a resource for each task with an "R."

• Identify who needs to approve or sign off on each task with a "✔."

• Identify who needs to be in the communication loop with a "C."

• Once the group has finished the chart, assess the appropriateness of lines of authority, responsibility, and communication, and make any necessary adjustments.

Select a facilitation tool that will help the group reach its objective.

Objective	Tools	Page
Provide focus	• Check-in • Agenda review	35 36
Build team cohesiveness	• Creating ground rules	38
Understand the situation	• Brainstorming • Brainwriting • Affinity process	54-55 56 57
Generate ideas	• Brainstorming • Brainwriting • Affinity process	54-55 56 57
Sort and prioritize	• Affinity process • Force field analysis	57 71
Plan action steps	• Flowchart • Tree diagram • Decision matrix • Contingency diagram	69 70 61 72
Decide	• Multi-voting • Decision matrix • Force field analysis • Quick-Check-Why	60 61 71 62

What If...	Try...
...I think the to-dos are too diffi-cult or complex for the group?	...breaking them down into manage-able chunks and ask more people to assist.
...the people who take responsi-bility are not the best people for the job?	...encouraging them to find a partner or mentor who will help them accomplish the task.
...the tool I chose is not accom-plishing what I had expected.	...being patient. Give the process time to produce the results. Explain the key steps of the process to the group.
...what if I am not proficient using a tool?	...practicing using the tool before introducing it to your group.
...the group gets derailed by unan-ticipated delays or unforeseen circumstances.	...engaging the group in contingency planning. Use troll search or force field analysis.

Pitfalls to avoid

✔ Lack of clarity about the specific actions that need to take place. Knowing WHO will "own" those actions and WHEN the actions will occur are critical to the successful completion of the group's task.

✔ Changing tools frequently. A group's productivity increases when they are knowledgeable and experienced with the use of a specific process.

✔ Assigning responsibilities to the GROUP. Assign tasks/responsibilities to a specific group member to ensure accountability.

✔ Failing to do contingency planning. Consider what could go wrong and the impact this would have on the group's work.

✔ Assigning responsibilities without consideration of factors such as workload, skill, knowledge level and interest in carrying out the task.

CHAPTER 7

DEALING WITH DIFFICULT BEHAVIORS

Topics covered by this chapter

■ How to use ground rules to minimize the impact of difficult behaviors.

■ What you can say and do when they occur in a meeting.

■ What to do in "conflict" situations.

Unproductive Behavior

Why it happens

Every group meeting gets sidetracked from time to time. It's generally *not* because anyone is trying to be difficult or sabotage the group's efforts. Rather, it's usually because the group didn't establish ground rules, or isn't doing a good job of honoring them. Often, it's just because someone isn't aware of how his or her behavior is affecting the group's ability to complete its work.

When it happens

A key to ensuring that the time a group spends together is *productive* time, is to establish ground rules and agree to stick to them. The group needs to reach consensus on the implications of breaking ground rules and agree to abide by its ground rules. (Enforcing ground rules is the group's job, not the facilitator's.) Ground rules not only help the group *prevent* distracting behavior, they provide guidelines for handling it.

Observing is one of the key skills which help facilitators keep meetings "moving and focused" (Chapter 4). As an objective facilitator, you are in an ideal position to spot difficult behaviors when they occur. Use your judgment about when to let something slide, when to wait for the group to address it, and when to step in.

Often, a reference to the team ground rules is all that's needed to curtail the behavior. Something as simple as a shift in eye contact or asking for input from another group member may do the trick, too.

Once you've decided that the situation requires you to step in, begin

HOW TO | *Enforce Ground Rules*

Often, we would rather sit quietly while someone behaves inappropriately (and hope someone else tells them!), rather than risk raising the discomfort level by talking to them about what they are doing. If participants collectively agree to share the responsibility of dealing with unproductive behavior, no individual needs to feel like the Ground Rules Police. The *group* is responsible for maintaining ground rules, *not* the facilitator or leader.

How to do it:

1. **Review** the ground rules frequently.

2. **Identify** behavior that you are concerned about.

3. **Suggest** a way for the group to get back on track.

Keep in mind that individuals who do not follow the ground rules are not necessarily troublemakers. If some members of your group seem to be "filibustering the airspace," it could be that they are very enthused about the topic and the work the group is doing, and want to participate. There are also people who are wired that way—they do their best thinking when they're engaged in discussion. Good ground rules can maximize everyone's effectiveness without anyone feeling stifled or ignored.

by sharing your non-judgmental observation with the group:

- "There seem to be several side conversations occurring, let's focus on one topic at a time."

- "Thank you for sharing your thoughts, let's see what others think about the situation."

Then let the individual(s) know how their behavior makes it difficult for the group to be as productive as it could be—and recommend an alternative behavior:

- "These side discussions are distracting to the people around you and are preventing you from participating fully in our group discussion. Can they wait until the break?"

- "We have a lot of people to hear from. Let me know if we've captured your main points on the chart here, and then I'd like to move on and let someone else have the chance to speak."

When Faced With...	Try...
The broken record	• Raising your hand: when they pause, break eye contact and ask for other people's thoughts. • Recording their comments or concerns on the flip chart, or adding them to the Parking Lot. • Jumping in with, "Thanks. Anyone else?" • Asking them if they are willing and able to "let go" of the particular concern so that the group can continue with the meeting.
The "gloom and doom" spokesperson	• Refocusing the discussion on the possible solutions, rather than on the problems. • Asking the group "does anyone else feel as strongly about this issue?" • Keeping them busy taking notes or writing on the flip chart. • Using humor: "that sounds terrible, how long has it been like that?" • Asking them to give at least one solution for each "problem" they identify. • Offering to discuss their concerns off line.
The interrupter	• Cutting it short: "Hold that thought, until we hear the rest of what John has to say." • Creating ground rules to control contributions (no interruptions, etc.) • Saying "thank you, however I would like to hear the end of Linda's comments…"

When Faced With...	Try...
The rambler	• Interrupting quickly and firmly.
	• Summarizing their key points, asking for confirmation that you've captured their thoughts, and then move on.
	• Saying "please take 10 seconds to complete your thought so we can hear from others."
	• Refocusing the discussion with a question or statement.
	• Directing your question at another group member.
	• Saying "that sounds like it would be a good item for discussion at break or lunch."
The side conversationalist	• Pausing, look at them and wait for them to stop.
	• Saying, "Let's get everyone on track."
	• Inviting them to join the group's discussion.
	• Asking if he/she has something to contribute to the group's discussion.
	• Saying, "let's make sure we are listening to what other members of the group have to say."

If the behavior continues, you may choose to talk with the person between meetings or during a break. Avoid blaming or labeling, and focus on solving the problem.

Working Through Conflict

Why it happens

Underlying most conflict is a challenge to someone's assumptions or expectations, coupled with an emotional response. Conflict is not necessarily a bad thing. It can stimulate communication among group members and result in clearer thinking and better decisions. Conflict is only a problem when a group doesn't know how to *manage* it, that is, when conflict is *mismanaged* in a way that fuels anxieties, stalls planning, or cripples future planning because of unresolved anger, frustration, or hurt.

When it happens

The key to using conflict productively is to plan for it. The more clearly spelled out the ground rules are for responding to this challenge, the less likely it will be that the emotional response will take over. Once the group has replaced *assumptions* with *agreements,* everyone will know what to expect from one another and there will be fewer conflicts to facilitate. And, when conflicts *do* arise, the group will have an agreed-upon understanding about how to manage them.

If it seems to you that the group's activities have moved beyond healthy debate into the realm of conflict, there are some ways you can help the group move through the process without losing the valuable insights that argument and strong feelings can bring to problem solving.

- Maintain your neutral position.

- Help the group be mindful of its ground rules.

- Intervene immediately if members launch into personal attacks.

- Let group members know they have been heard by paraphrasing and summarizing the points of view being expressed.

- Check in often with group members to make sure they feel they have been heard correctly and feel understood.

- Work with the group to expand participants' understanding of one another's viewpoints, for example, through:

➤ Role playing – inviting group members to "try on" one another's arguments.

➤ Force-fitting – asking group members to take an idea they disagree with and modifying it to make it work.

➤ Analyzing – encouraging group members to identify the core value in their argument. Ask if they think the group is missing this point.

Don't be afraid to call a break if you need time to plan your approach to facilitate the conflict – or if members of the group just need to cool down.

Additional Resources on Conflict

There are many useful resources that address the topic of conflict. Here are some that you may find helpful:

Borisoff, D, and Victor, D.A. *Conflict management: A communication skills approach* (2nd ed.). Boston, Mass.: Allyn & Bacon, 1997.

Mayer, B.S. *The dynamics of conflict resolution: A practitioner's guide.* San Francisco, Calif.: Jossey-Bass, 2000.

Schwarz, R. *Facilitating difficult conversations.* Chapel Hill, N.C.: Roger Schwarz & Associates, IAF conference 2001.

Mayer, R.J. *Conflict management: the courage to confront.* Columbus, Ohio: Battelle Press, 1995.

Pitfalls to avoid

✔ Underestimating the power of ground rules. Although they may appear to be simple, they provide an effective way of addressing problematic behaviors.

✔ Hoping that someone else will deal with inappropriate behavior. The facilitator's role is to address behavior problems soon after it occurs.

✔ Rewarding individuals for "not doing what they are supposed to do" (i.e. allowing side conversations to continue). Inconsistent application of ground rules will ultimately make application of them difficult and possibly ineffective.

✔ Confusing "conflict" and meaningful discussion. Differences of opinion are not necessarily synonymous with conflict. It is often the difference of opinion, which provides valuable insights.

✔ Feeling that you have to referee every disagreement. This assumes that all disagreements need mediation, and your intervention may prohibit the group from resolving their own issues.

Rojong (pronounced ROY-yong)

An Indonesian word meaning "the relationship among a group of people committed to accomplishing a task of mutual benefit."

INDEX

-A-
Affinity Process.................................57
Agenda................25, 26, 36, 43, 45
Assignments 40
Attendance.................................39

-B-
Balancing.............................24, 42
Brainstorming.......................54, 55
Brainwriting.............................56

-C-
Check In.....................................35
Check Out..................................45
Clarifying....................................42
Closing..45
Conflict................................82, 83
Consensus.............................58, 59
Contingency Planning................70
Creativity....................................53

-D-
Decision Matrix....................61, 73
Difficult Behaviors......................78

-E-
Equipment..................................27
Evaluation.....................................9

-F-
Feedback.....................................68
Force Field Analysis....................71

-G-
Goals...17
Ground Rules........38, 39, 40, 41, 79
Group Leader..............................14

-I-
Idea Generation....................52, 53
Implementation...........................68
Interruptions...............................39

-L-
Logistics......................................27

-M-
Milestones...................................17
Multi-Voting..........................59, 60

-O-
Objectives...................................25
Observing................................8, 42

-P-
Parking Lot.................................43
Participation..................................7
Problem Solving..........................16
Promptness.................................39

-Q-
Quick-Check-Why.................62, 63

-R-
Recorder......................................36
Room Set-up...............................28
Round-Robin..............................55

-S-
Sponsor.......................................14
Stimulating............................42, 53
Summary.....................................43

-T-
Teleconferencing.........................46
Timekeeper.................................37
Tree Diagram.........................69, 70
Troll Search............................70, 71

HOWICK ASSOCIATES

HOWICK ASSOCIATES is an organizational development and training firm, established in 1984. Through the years we have worked with over 500 clients, helping them enhance their performance at the organizational, team and individual leader levels. A critical aspect of our work is about changing the quality of conversations in an organization. A simple, yet challenging concept. High-quality conversations help people consider alternatives, align their efforts, discover new learning opportunities, make higher quality decisions and honestly evaluate their progress. One of the most effective methods for accomplishing these results is through carefully designed, thoughtfully organized, well facilitated meetings. We believe it is one of the most important components for accomplishing real sustainable change.

Facilitation is a core practice of the work we do in:

- Team Effectiveness

- Leadership Development

- Organizational and 360-degree feedback

- Large Group and Whole Systems Change

ORDER TODAY!

ONLY $32.95

YES! Send me The NEW Compleat Facilitator:

Name _____

Organization _____

Title _____

Address _____

City_____ State_____ Zip_____

Phone (_____) _____

The NEW Compleat Facilitator: $32.95

_____ 1-5 copies ($32.95 each) _____

_____ 6-10 copies ($29.95 each) _____

_____11-19 copies ($26.95 each)_____

_____ 20 or more ($23.95 each) _____

Subtotal _____

Postage and Handling

Single copy add $4.65 _____

For each additional add $1.75 _____

Wisconsin residents please apply
appropriate sales tax (varies by county) _____

Total _____

FREE SHIPPING: *For orders of more than 20 copies,
HOWICK ASSOCIATES will pay the postage and handling.
For international orders please call 1-800-236-3370*

Payment: ☐ Check Enclosed ☐ VISA ☐ Mastercard Card #_____ Exp. Date _____

Card Holder's Signature _____

Mail to: **HOWICK ASSOCIATES** • 111 N. Fairchild St. • Madison, WI 53703 • 800-236-3370 • FAX 608-233-1194

- -

ORDER TODAY!

ONLY $32.95

YES! Send me The NEW Compleat Facilitator:

Name _____

Organization _____

Title _____

Address _____

City_____ State_____ Zip_____

Phone (_____) _____

The NEW Compleat Facilitator: $32.95

_____ 1-5 copies ($32.95 each) _____

_____ 6-10 copies ($29.95 each) _____

_____11-19 copies ($26.95 each)_____

_____ 20 or more ($23.95 each) _____

Subtotal _____

Postage and Handling

Single copy add $4.65 _____

For each additional add $1.75 _____

Wisconsin residents please apply
appropriate sales tax (varies by county) _____

Total _____

FREE SHIPPING: *For orders of more than 20 copies,
HOWICK ASSOCIATES will pay the postage and handling.
For international orders please call 1-800-236-3370*

Payment: ☐ Check Enclosed ☐ VISA ☐ Mastercard Card #_____ Exp. Date _____

Card Holder's Signature _____

Mail to: **HOWICK ASSOCIATES** • 111 N. Fairchild St. • Madison, WI 53703 • 800-236-3370 • FAX 608-233-1194